DRONES
EYES IN THE SKIES

POLICE
DRONES

DANIEL R. FAUST

PowerKiDS
press.

New York

Published in 2016 by The Rosen Publishing Group, Inc.
29 East 21st Street, New York, NY 10010

First Edition

Editor: Sarah Machajewski
Book Design: Reann Nye

Photo Credits: Cover, p. 1 Slavoljub Pantelic/Shutterstock.com; p. 5 Maria Dryfhout/Shutterstock.com; p. 6 funkyfrogstock/Shutterstock.com; p. 7 The Washington Post/Getty Images; p. 8 https://commons. wikimedia.org/wiki/File-Black_Hornet_Nano_Helicopter_UAV.jpg; p. 9 THOMAS SAMSON/AFP/ Getty Images; p. 11 https://upload.wikimedia.org/wikipedia/commons/2/24/KD2C_Skeet_drone.jpg; p. 13 JUAN MABROMATA/AFP/Getty Images; p. 14 RedDaxLuma/Shutterstock.com; p.15 Don Ryan/ AP Images; p. 17 (map) Volina/Shutterstock.com; p. 17 (background) mexrix/Shutterstock.com; p. 19 Dale G. Young/AP Images; p. 20 Newnow/Shutterstock.com; p. 21 Scott Olson/ Getty Images News/Getty Images; p. 23 pisaphotography/Shutterstock.com; p. 25 ROBYN BECK/ AFP/Getty Images; p. 27 RJ Sangosti/Denver Post/Getty Images; p. 29 Alexander Kolomietz/ Shutterstock.com; p. 30 B.Stefanov/Shutterstock.com.

Library of Congress Cataloging-in-Publication Data

Names: Faust, Daniel R.
Title: Police drones / Daniel R. Faust.
Description: New York : PowerKids Press, 2016. | Series: Drones: eyes in the skies | Includes index.
Identifiers: ISBN 9781508145004 (pbk.) | ISBN 9781508145011 (6 pack) | ISBN 9781508145028 (library bound)
Subjects: LCSH: Drone aircraft–Juvenile literature. | Aeronautics in police work–Juvenile literature.
Classification: LCC UG1242.D7 F38 2016 | DDC 623.74'69–dc23

Manufactured in the United States of America

CPSIA Compliance Information: Batch #BW16PK: For Further Information contact Rosen Publishing, New York, New York at 1-800-237-9932

CONTENTS

INTRODUCING DRONES

Drones, or unmanned aerial **vehicles** (UAVs), are aircraft designed to operate without a human pilot on board. A drone is usually controlled by a human operator using a remote control or by a preprogrammed flight computer, which is known as autonomous flying.

You've probably heard a lot about drones. The United States military and militaries around the world use drones to carry out important missions. Militaries use drones because they can fly over dangerous, or unsafe, areas without risking the lives of human pilots.

Recently, drones have become popular among private citizens and businesses. Drones flown for fun or for business purposes must follow federal rules. Some government agencies, such as the Central **Intelligence** Agency (CIA), Federal Bureau of Investigation (FBI), and Department of Homeland Security also use drones. This book will focus on drones used by law enforcement agencies.

The U.S. military has used drones for more than 40 years. Civilians, or nonmilitary people, have just recently started using drones, such as the one pictured here, for fun.

DECONSTRUCTING DRONE PARTS

Whether drones carry military equipment or just a digital camera, they're built and operated using the same basic principles. Drones are commonly made of plastics and lightweight metals, such as aluminum. Power is provided by batteries or another kind of fuel cell. Some companies are developing solar-powered drones, which would work using the sun's energy.

FLY BY WIFI

Some drones have special software that allows them to be controlled by smartphone or tablet. Operators can even stream live video from the drone's camera directly to the mobile device.

Smaller drones are operated by handheld remote controls. Larger drones are controlled from command stations that look much like the cockpit of an airplane.

Drones are equipped with simple navigational equipment, such as GPS. Drones are also equipped with cameras and other **sensors** to help pilots operate them safely. A flight controller, which is also called autopilot, is a simple computer that acts as the drone's "brain." Some flight controllers can be programmed to fly the drone along a preset path. Depending on the drone, operators use small handheld controllers, portable computers, or large command stations to control its flight.

MANY TYPES OF DRONES

Drones come in many shapes and sizes. Some drones are small enough to fit in your pocket or in the palm of your hand, while others are as large as an airplane. Many of the drones used by the U.S. government and military resemble regular aircraft. The drones you can buy at a hobby store are commonly quadcopters. This name comes from the four **rotors** they use to fly. Drones can have six or eight rotors, too.

Today, regular people, journalists, businesses, and movie studios are using drones. Major companies such as Google and Amazon want to use drones to deliver packages and provide Internet service. Police departments and prisons are using drones to enforce the law, track fugitives, and more.

DRONE SIZES

The Black Hornet Nano is a quadcopter that's only 2 inches (5.1 cm) across. The RQ-4 Global Hawk has a **wingspan** of 131 feet (40 m), making it one of the largest drones in the world.

NANO DRONE

Police climb an apartment building during a rescue mission while a drone flies nearby. In the future, police may be able to use drones to see what's happening inside hard-to-reach places where they're needed.

FROM THE MILITARY TO THE PUBLIC

Drone **technology** was first developed for the military. The earliest drones were self-propelled torpedoes that dropped from airplanes during World War I and World War II. During the Cold War, advances in technology allowed aircraft to be flown remotely. They were used to take detailed photographs or record video.

At the beginning of the 21st century, the U.S. military used drones to survey battlefields, gather information, locate enemy forces, and track targets. Law enforcement agencies soon started using drones to do the same. Currently, only a handful of U.S. agencies are allowed to fly drones in American airspace. For example, the U.S. Customs and Border Protection regularly uses drones to patrol America's borders.

TARGET PRACTICE

The earliest drones were small, radio-controlled aircraft used to train pilots and gunners. In less than 50 years, drones went from being targets to finding targets of their own.

First used in 1945, the Skeet was a radio-controlled drone developed by the U.S. Navy. Skeet drones were used as target practice to help train naval gunners.

DRONES OVER AMERICA

The skies above the United States are regulated by the Federal Aviation Administration, or FAA. One of the FAA's jobs is to make sure all airports and aircraft operate safely, including drones.

Under the FAA's current laws, anyone can fly a drone for fun. In order to fly a drone in the United States for other purposes, you must receive official permission from the FAA. Whether you fly a drone for fun or for profit, everyone must follow the FAA's rules. One rule states that people can only fly drones during the day. Drones must not fly higher than 400 feet (122 m). Drones must remain in sight of their operator at all times and avoid airports, private property, and other aircraft. Law enforcement agencies have to follow these rules, too.

Safety is important when it comes to drones. The FAA requires all drones to stay away from manned aircraft, such as helicopters. However, pilots have been reporting that drones are getting in the way of flying safely, which may lead the FAA to change its rules.

POLICE DRONES AND THE FAA

If a law enforcement agency wants to use a drone, it must get permission from the FAA. However, this isn't always easy. The FAA has been slow to approve the use of drones over American cities because of the obvious safety issues. Drones aren't perfect technology, and an out-of-control drone over a populated city could be dangerous to both people and property.

The earliest drones used by American law enforcement agencies were owned by the government. In the 1980s, police departments used drones to track people they thought were committing crimes. In 2014, it was reported that the U.S. Customs and Border Protection used its **fleet** of drones to carry out more than 700 **surveillance** missions between 2010 and 2012. They were working on behalf of other federal, state, and local law enforcement agencies.

DRONES ABOVE

WARNING

Government agencies, such as the Department of Homeland Security and U.S. Customs and Border Protection, often lend drones to smaller police departments to help with investigations.

Once police departments figured out they could use drones to assist with their work, many wanted to put the technology to use. The Mesa County Sheriff's Department in Colorado has been using drones since January 2010. It has used drones for search-and-rescue missions and hopes to one day use drones to track wildfires.

In 2015, the FAA authorized the Michigan State Police to be the first law enforcement agency to operate drones throughout an entire state. The state police plan to use drones to assist officers during search-and-rescue missions or after accidents and natural disasters.

More police departments want to start using drones, but it's not easy to get approval. There's a lot of paperwork and time involved in getting the FAA's permission to fly drones.

RIGHT OR WRONG?

Law enforcement's use of drones can be very **controversial**, as many people are uncomfortable with the idea of being monitored by drones.

POLICE DEPARTMENTS WITH DRONE PERMITS

Washington
Oregon
Idaho
Montana
North Dakota
Minnesota
Wisconsin
Michigan
Vermont
Maine
New Hampshire
New York
Massachusetts
Rhode Island
Connecticut
Wyoming
South Dakota
Iowa
Pennsylvania
New Jersey
Delaware
Maryland
Washington, D.C.
Nevada
Utah
Nebraska
Illinois
Indiana
Ohio
West Virginia
Virginia
Colorado
Kansas
Missouri
Kentucky
North Carolina
California
Arizona
Oklahoma
Arkansas
Tennessee
South Carolina
New Mexico
Mississippi
Alabama
Georgia
Texas
Louisiana
Florida

O DRONE PERMIT

More police departments apply for drone permits each year. This map shows how many police departments are already allowed to use drones.

DRONES USED BY LAW ENFORCEMENT

Companies began producing and selling drones as more everyday people became interested in them. These drones, which started as toys, were soon being purchased by police departments across the country. Many of these drones, like the DJI Phantom, are the same as the kinds of drones available to recreational flyers. Others, such as the Vanguard ShadowHawk or the AeroVironment Qube, were made with the needs of law enforcement in mind.

Like hobby drones, police drones can carry pretty much anything the user wants. This raises many questions about safety and privacy, and some people have taken action to keep police drones under control. In 2015, a bill passed in North Dakota that said police can't arm drones with lethal, or deadly, weapons. However, the bill doesn't outlaw the carrying of weapons such as tear gas or rubber bullets. The way police will use drones is a concern many people share.

Many of the drones currently used by the police are no different from the ones you can buy from the store.

MANHUNT!

You've probably heard stories about the military using drones to hunt for enemies in foreign lands. Did you know that law enforcement does the same thing in the United States? Police agencies use drones to help identify criminals and locate fugitives.

A drone can be used to fly over an area where a suspected criminal may be. A drone can circle over the area for hours, gathering real-time video surveillance. Drones that carry special cameras (including those that can see motion in the dark) can help the police identify their targets in the wilderness, in bad weather, and at night.

It could take police officers days or even months to search everywhere a criminal might be hiding. Drones allow the police to search a large area in less time, which helps them get dangerous people off the streets more quickly.

Because the human body gives off heat, drones with heat sensors can be used to find people who are hiding or on the run. Drones can do this work more quickly and less expensively than other kinds of aircraft used by police departments.

SEARCH AND RESCUE

Police departments can use drones to locate more than just criminals—they can also be used to find people who are lost or hurt. The same equipment that helps drones locate criminals can also be used to find lost hikers, runaways, and other missing people.

Drones may be more practical than human search parties. A single drone can search several miles in a matter of minutes, while it would take a human search party several hours. Unlike people, drones can search day and night. They can also see through clouds, rain, and fog. In addition, drones can be used to deliver food, water, medical supplies, and cell phones to people in hard-to-reach places. Drones are even being used as aerial lifeguards, locating swimmers in distress and delivering life preservers when needed.

LOST AND FOUND

Drones aren't just being used to help find lost people. Some people have even started using drones to find lost pets and track and rescue stray dogs and cats.

Drones are helpful during search-and-rescue missions, especially in wilderness areas such as forests and mountains. Their bird's-eye view can save hours of searching.

WHEN DISASTER STRIKES

The first men and women to arrive at the scene of an accident or natural disaster are known as first responders. First responders are usually police officers, firefighters, paramedics, or emergency medical technicians. They're often the first people to locate and help victims at the scene.

After a disaster such as a building collapse or earthquake, drones can be used to survey the area and search for survivors. Because drones are small and highly **maneuverable**, they can be sent into spaces that are too small for larger aircraft. Water and other supplies can be delivered to people who are trapped. Drones can also be used to determine when it's safe to send in first responders. Several police departments across the United States are using drones to locate and fight wildfires, too.

IN THE LINE OF FIRE

In 2015, it was reported that drones were getting in the way of efforts to fight wildfires. Drones flying over and recording the fires got in the way of aircraft that were attempting to fly in to help.

Drones have been used to help locate survivors of natural disasters, such as floods and earthquakes. Because of their small size, drones can search places that helicopters and other vehicles can't.

KEEPING AN EYE ON THINGS

Some of the earliest uses for drones were aerial photography and surveillance. Police departments are interested in using drones in the same way. As "eyes in the skies," drones can provide valuable information to police officers on the ground.

Police departments can use drones to gather information about an area before sending officers into a potentially dangerous situation. Law enforcement agencies can use drones for crowd or traffic control, as well as to search crowds for people suspected of a crime or persons of interest. Drones can be used to photograph crime scenes and search for evidence. Drones can also be used to take aerial photographs of accident sites or to clear debris from blocked roads and highways. They can even be used to gather information to help figure out how crimes and accidents happened.

Police departments are not only using drones to locate traffic accidents, but they're also using them to help reconstruct the events leading up to the accident.

POLICE DRONES AND YOUR RIGHTS

The FAA's drone safety rules don't cover topics such as privacy and civil rights. Many people worry that police departments might use drones to illegally spy on **law-abiding** citizens. As of 2015, only 14 states have privacy laws that keep the police from using drones to spy on citizens without first obtaining a **warrant**. Lawmakers have repeatedly tried to pass national legislation that would protect people from having police drones invade their privacy without cause.

Some groups, such as the American Civil Liberties Union (ACLU), are worried that increased drone use by law enforcement agencies could lead to a future where the police use drones to track citizens. The information could be used to create a database of someone's daily routine. Others claim that increased drone use would benefit privacy by creating a demand for greater privacy rights.

The thought of drones silently flying over our cities and gathering data about private citizens concerns many people. It's important to find the balance between safety and privacy.

THE FUTURE OF POLICE DRONES

Science-fiction movies and television shows often portray a future where the skies are patrolled by law enforcement robots. Although more police departments are applying for drone permits from the FAA every year, it's unlikely that this fiction will ever become fact.

Just as hobby and commercial drones are becoming more popular, domestic law enforcement agencies will likely continue to use these amazing machines. Technological advances will lead to drones that can fly higher, faster, and further than the drones that exist today. Better cameras and sensors could lead to police drones that could locate a criminal in a crowded building. One day there could even be drones that could collect and analyze evidence from a crime scene. We don't yet know what the future holds.

GLOSSARY

controversial: Causing people to disagree or argue.

fleet: Ships, aircraft, or vehicles that operate together.

intelligence: Information that is of military or political value.

law-abiding: Following the law.

maneuverable: Able to change position easily.

rotor: The hub and rotating blade that supply lift for a rotorcraft, such as a helicopter.

sensor: A machine that measures a physical property, such as movement or heat, and records or responds to it.

surveillance: Close observation.

technology: The way people do something using tools and the tools they use.

vehicle: A machine that is powered to move on its own.

warrant: A document given by a judge or the government that allows the police or other law enforcement agency to make an arrest, search private property, or enforce laws.

wingspan: The measurement from the tip of one wing to the tip of the other.

INDEX

WEBSITES

Due to the changing nature of Internet links, PowerKids Press has developed an online list of websites related to the subject of this book. This site is updated regularly. Please use this link to access the list: www.powerkidslinks.com/dron/poli